WATER OVER THE FALLS

101 of the Most Memorable Events at Niagara Falls

By
Paul Gromosiak
© 2006

Above Photo: John Penrod
Cover Photo: Ron Paré

What a place! What a history! Niagara Falls and the river which created them have been the scene of many interesting and exciting natural and human events, from the end of the Ice Age, 12,500 years ago, to today. It was quite a challenge to select 100 of the most memorable incidents, since Niagara's history is replete with a myriad of events. The process was made easier because of the six summers I spent answering questions about the falls from visitors to Niagara Reservation State Park.

This book is divided into eleven sections, each of which lists incidents in reverse chronology. The numerical order does not in any way imply the level of importance of each event.

Enjoy!

Contents

View of the Falls from the Canadian side.

Prospect Point

American Falls
260M (850Ft)

Luna Island
30.5M (100Ft)

Bridal Veil Falls
15M (50Ft)

Goat Island

Terrapin Point

Canadian Horseshoe Falls
670 M (2200Ft)

Low Level
57M (188Ft)

High Level
54M (177Ft)

21-34M (70-110Ft)

Cave of the Winds

Journey Behind The Falls

USA
Canada

Niagara River
56.6M (185Ft)

Niagara's Notable Daredevils

One

At 9 A.M., Sunday, June 18, 1995, Steve Trotter, 32, the same man who went over alone in 1985, and his female companion, Lori Martin, 29, became the first male/female duo to successfully ride a barrel over the Horseshoe Falls. They had to be rescued from the rocks just below the falls, an extremely dangerous accomplishment by Canadian authorities.

The 1,100-pound barrel was constructed of two water heaters welded together and wrapped in several layers of fiberglass, foam and Kevlar. Painted on the side of the white 10-foot-long capsule were slogans including "The Cowboys from Hell" and "Take the Real Plunge."

Both Trotter and Martin were relatively uninjured, but they were arrested and faced heavy fines.

Two

At 8:35 A.M., on Sunday, September 26, 1993, Dave Munday, a 56-year-old mechanic from Caistor Centre, Ontario, made his second trip over the Horseshoe Falls. His $500 660-pound converted plastic and aluminum diving bell, painted red and white, made its plunge near the Table Rock observation area on the Canadian side of the river. He became the first person to go over the Horseshoe Falls twice.

Munday described his ride as "wild." He was shaken up and suffered a few bruises on his face and shoulders. He was also bleeding from where he had bitten his tongue.

He dedicated his feat to all men over fifty and lovers of low-tech daredevils. He also said he did it to spite some reporters who accused him of cushioning his first plunge by using a high-tech barrel.

The first time he was asked if he would ever go over the falls again, he replied, "that's it!" Later on, even after paying a $6,000 fine, he said he would like to try the American Falls the next time. Most people consider a ride over that falls to be extremely dangerous because of the large amount of talus (pile of rock) there.

Three

At about 2 P.M., on Tuesday, June 5, 1990, Jessie W. Sharp, a 28-year-old from Tennessee, died when he rode a polyethylene kayak, named "Rapidman," over the Horseshoe Falls.

When he was spotted in the Canadian Rapids, Ontario Hydro officials tried to lower the water using the water control gates located just above the rapids. Intent on reaching the waterfall, Sharp was able to avoid the shallow places. He also carefully maneuvered around the many boulders scattered all over. As he went over the falls, perhaps as a triumphant salute, he lifted his arms and oars above his head.

The kayak, only slightly damaged, was recovered the same afternoon. Jessie's body was never found.

Jessie was an experienced kayaker. He thought he would not only survive going over the falls, but also the ride through the treacherous rapids in the gorge. So confident was he that he had made reservations for dinner that night in a Niagara Falls, Ontario restaurant.

Four

At about 5:30 P.M., on Wednesday, September 27, 1989, Peter DeBernadi, 42, of Niagara Falls, Ontario, and his partner, Jeffrey J. Petkovich, 24, of Ottawa, became the first pair to go over the Horseshoe Falls and survive. Their 3,000-pound converted 12-foot tank contained two compartments, hammocks with automobile seat belts, plexiglass windows and a video camera to record the trip.

Neither man suffered serious injuries. They said they did it "to fight drugs; there's a lot better things for kids to do than be on the brink of dope — go over the brink of the falls; you'll see what a high is all about."

Petkovich had apparently had enough of stunting at the Falls for one lifetime. DeBernardi, however, was determined to go on risking his life. On Tuesday, August 15, 1990, he was arrested by U.S. Border Patrol agents when he came to Niagara Falls, New York with a suspicious-looking huge yellow doughnut-shaped barrel on a flatbed truck. He planned to do the unthinkable — go over the American Falls.

He was deported and told not to return to the United States for five years. He vowed to return someday and make the perilous plunge.

In an attempt to gain media attention to his resentment of the ordinances against stunting by the falls, DeBernardi made an attempt to go out on one of the cables of the Spanish Aerocar on Sunday, September 9, 1990. Using a harness, he planned to go out to the middle of the cable and hang a Canadian flag directly over the Whirlpool. The authorities thwarted this demonstration and fined DeBernardi $503. The Canadian Provincial Court also gave him a stern warning to put an end to his Falls follies.

Five

On Sunday, July 28, 1985, Dave Munday failed in his first effort to go over the Horseshoe Falls in a barrel. Police were able to trap him above the falls in a hydropower pool. He was fined $503 in the Ontario Provincial Court. He was also placed on a two-year probation which, if violated, could bring up to 30 days in jail and a $1,000 fine. "The only thing that bothers me," he commented, "is that I'd never been arrested in my life. This is a whole new ballgame, being treated almost like a criminal."

Irrespective of the warnings from the authorities, Munday made a successful trip over the Horseshoe Falls on the morning of Saturday, October 5, 1985. Besides a two-way radio, the sophisticated red and white barrel contained an oxygen tank and an inside-mounted video camera.

The only injury Munday suffered was to his wallet. He was fined $1,500. He was lucky that he was not incarcerated.

Six

At about 8 A.M., on Sunday, August 18, 1985, Steven Trotter, 22, from Rhode Island, went over the Horseshoe Falls near Terrapin Point. His barrel was made from modified pickle barrels lined inside with the same foam packing used to ship nuclear warheads. "It was like an elevator with no cable," he said of the 170-foot plunge. He suffered only a sore back and bruised elbow.

He had aspirations to become a professional stuntman, so he thought a successful ride over the falls would give his career "a boost." He did make some money from advertisers and selling tee shirts. He even appeared on the Tonight Show with Johnny Carson. Unfortunately for him, he was not accepted into the stunters' school that he wanted to attend.

Seven

On the morning of June 11, 1977, Karel Soucek, 30, from Hamilton, Ontario, rode a 300-pound discarded oil tank, equipped with a bucket seat, light bulbs, and a citizens band radio, through the Whirlpool Rapids. In order to rescue him, Canadian authorities used a helicopter to force Soucek's barrel to the shore of the Whirlpool.

His experience riding the rapids convinced him he could successfully go over the Horseshoe Falls. So, on Monday, July 2, 1984, Soucek went over the mighty falls in a bright red plastic barrel which bore his name and the slogan, "Last of Niagara's Daredevils." His only injury was a cut on his forehead. It's surprising that his nerves were not frayed, as being stuck for awhile in a falling enclosed space. Years before, he was very upset when trapped in an elevator in the Niagara Falls, New York, public library.

Soucek was fined $500 in the Ontario Provincial Court, but he didn't care. Unlike other daredevils, he was convinced he would make a lot of money from sales of a video of his trip and a book about daredevils.

He also thought he would make a killing recreating his stunt in public arenas. Sadly, his first attempt was his last. He died from severe injuries when his wooden barrel fell 180 feet and struck the side of a water tank, during a Thrill Show and Destruction Derby at the Houston Astrodome.

Above Photo From: Niagara – *River of Fame*, The Kiwanis Club of Stamford, Ont., Inc. 1968, 1986.

Karel Soucek displays his confidence with his thumb up.

Eight

At about 6 A.M., on Wednesday, June 4, 1975, Henri J. Rechatin, his wife, Janyck, and a friend, Frank Lucas, went over the Whirlpool on one of the cables of the Spanish Aero Car, a distance of about 1,800 feet. Henri stood on top of a fork-like device attached to the rear of a motorcycle, balancing everything and everyone with a long pole. Lucas drove the cycle, while Henri's wife dangled precariously one foot below the cycle and 170 feet above the spinning, churning water. Well greased and jointed, it was no easy task moving on the cable.

In 1994, Rechatin expressed a desire to celebrate the 20th anniversary of his Whirlpool stunt. This time, he hoped to cross the gorge on a tightrope. He was not given permission to perform because of concerns about crowd control and safety.

Nine

At about 11 A.M., on July 15, 1961, William Fitzgerald, alias Nathan Boya, 29, went over the Horseshoe Falls in a ball he called "The Plunge-o-sphere," which was six feet in diameter and made of a steel framework covered with rubber. He was the first African-American to go over the waterfalls in a barrel. Even though he was "scared stiff," he suffered only a few cuts and bruises. He paid a fine of $113.

Why did Fitzgerald do it? His reasons ranged from an attempt to prove his love for a French woman to gathering material for a novel. He later stated that it was really the culmination of a boyhood goal. Whatever his reason, unlike the other daredevils, he never sought fame or fortune.

Ten

At 3:03 P.M., on Sunday, August 5, 1951, a famous local riverman and daredevil, William "Red" Hill Jr., 38, went over the Horseshoe Falls in his "Thing," nothing more than a series of 13 graduated truck tire inner tubes bound together by an interlacing net arrangement and canvas straps. His friends and family, as well as the authorities, tried to talk him out of the feat, but Red was determined to do what his equally famous father, "Red" Hill Sr., had wanted to do, but didn't.

A terrible silence came over the more than 200,000 spectators when they saw pieces of the "Thing" come floating, one by one, to the surface of the river just below the falls. Hill's badly battered body was recovered the following morning in an eddy below the Canadian Maid of the Mist boat landing.

Since Hill's death, regulations against stunting by the falls have been stiffened by both Canadian and American authorities, much to no avail.

Eleven

At 3:35 P.M., on Saturday, July 5, 1930, George L. Stathakis, 46, an author and philosopher from Buffalo, sought fame, fortune, and truth by going over the Horseshoe Falls in an oak one-ton heavily reinforced barrel. He wanted to make money for his literary pursuits by selling the motion picture rights for his trip. He also planned an extensive lecturing tour. He survived the plunge unscathed, but his 3-hour supply of oxygen ran out after the force of the falling water kept his barrel submerged for more than sixteen hours.

Along for the ride, was Stathakis' pet 103-year-old turtle, "Sonny Boy," which Stathakis claimed was held sacred by an unnamed Greek cult. The reptile survived. Before the stunt, Stathakis told reporters that if he didn't survive, his turtle would someday reveal the secret of the trip "at the proper time." As far as it is known, Sonny Boy never uttered a word.

Twelve

On July 4, 1928, Joseph Albert "Jean" Lussier, 37, a French Canadian, went over the Horseshoe Falls in a 1,037 pound rubber ball built around 2 steel frame pieces. He survived quite well and went on to profit a little from the venture. He took his ball on tours, where he showed movies and told about the experience.

In the 1950's, he talked about going over the American Falls in another rubber ball, if someone would pay him $10,000. Lucky for him, his dream never came true. For certainly, it would have been a nightmare.

Thirteen

At about 8:55 A.M., on Sunday, July 11, 1920, Charles Stephens, a 58-year-old barber from Bristol, England, went over the Horseshoe Falls in an oak barrel weighing 600 pounds. A blacksmith's anvil and other lead weights lined the bottom of the barrel for ballast. Stephens made the plunge so he could stop being a barber. He planned to make a lot of money by giving lectures and showing his barrel all over England.

"But suppose you don't come back," asked a reporter before the stunt. "No use supposin'," answered Stephens, adding, "you does it or you doesn't. I bet I does."

Well, he didn't. Pieces of his poorly constructed barrel kept washing ashore below the falls throughout the day. The next morning, a complete right arm was taken from the river at the Canadian Maid of the Mist landing. On the arm was a tatoo which was identified by Stephen's widow. That and a piece of his rib were all that the river returned of the stunter's remains.

Fourteen

On July 25, 1911, the first man to go over the Horseshoe Falls in a barrel survived. Bobby Leach, from Niagara Falls, New York, went over in a newly-built steel barrel. He was quite battered and bleeding when rescuers pulled him through the hatch. That same year, he had had more luck performing two other stunts. On April 21, he parachuted into the river from the Falls View Bridge. On June 28, he made a trip through the Whirlpool Rapids in another steel barrel.

In 1926, Leach went to New Zealand on a vaudeville tour. While walking down an Auckland street, he slipped on an orange peel, breaking his leg. The leg became infected so badly that it had to be amputated. Leach died from shock during the operation.

Reacting to what seemed to be a classic case of irony, someone from Plainfield, New Jersey, wrote the following poem.

"Now this is the story of brave Bobby Leach,
Who tried every stunt that a mortal could reach.
He conquered Niagara, rapids and falls,
Balloon-borne, he weathered the wind's wildest squalls —
Until, like Achilles, old fate found his heel
He died from a slip on a stray orange peel."

Fifteen

In the afternoon of Tuesday, June 27, 1911, Lincoln J. Beachy, a 24-year-old Californian, took off in a biplane from a field in the city of Niagara Falls, New York. He flew to the Canadian Rapids and right over the brink of the Horseshoe Falls. Then he descended deep into the gorge and went under the arches of the Falls View Bridge. About 20,000 spectators witnessed the stunt.

When asked about the flight, Beachy said, "it was a flight filled with more dangers than you can imagine. The spray cut my face so hard that I had to close my eyes as I made the dip, and they were shut when I passed under the bridge. I was never in such treacherous air currents."

On March 14, 1915, at the Panama-Pacific Exhibition, in San Francisco, Beachy was killed when his German Taube monoplane crashed into San Francisco Bay.

Sixteen

In the summer of 1910, Oscar Williams made several crossings of the gorge on a wire. By that time, public interest in tightrope or wire walking had pretty much petered out. Only small crowds watched William's performances.

Above Photo From: Niagara Falls, NY Public Library

Annie Taylor standing by the barrel she rode over the Horseshoe Falls.

Seventeen

At 4:23 P.M., on Thursday, October 24, 1901, Annie Edson Taylor, a widowed schoolteacher from Bay City, Michigan, and many other places, celebrated her 46th birthday (so she said) by going over the Horseshoe Falls in a leaking 160-pound oak barrel. At her feet, to keep the barrel upright, was a 100-pound anvil. All Annie suffered was a terrible fright and a cut on her forehead. She was the first person to perform such a stunt at the falls.

When asked if she would ever go over the falls again, Annie said, "if it was with my dying breath, I would caution anyone against attempting the feat. I will never go over the falls again. I would sooner walk up to the mouth of a cannon knowing it was going to blow me to pieces than make another trip over the falls."

Annie went over the falls for one simple reason — to make money. She had debts to pay, and she was deathly afraid of ending up in the poorhouse in her old age. Sadly, things never went well for her. The agent she hired absconded with her barrel, displaying it with a younger and prettier "Annie Taylor" in many cities. Annie had a replica of her barrel made and went on a speaking circuit. People didn't find her to be an interesting speaker, so she had to give that up. She ended up back in Niagara Falls, New York, selling mementoes of her stunt to tourists. She became ill and ended up in the Niagara County Infirmary, where she died on April 29, 1921, the poor woman she never wanted to be. A collection was taken up to give her a decent burial. She rests in Oakwood Cemetery in Niagara Falls, New York.

Eighteen

On September 7, 1901, Maude Willard rode a barrel through the Whirlpool Rapids. With her was her pet fox terrier. The barrel drifted in the Whirlpool's dangerous waters for hours. In the meantime, the canine's snout became stuck in the craft's only airhole, suffocating poor Ms. Willard. It took rescuers some time to get hold of the barrel.

Ms Willard was supposed to be joined at the Whirlpool by the dare-devil, Carlisle Graham, who would swim alongside her barrel all the way to Lewiston. Their duet was going to be filmed.

Nineteen

On September 6, 1901, Martha E. Wagenfuhrer made a successful trip through the Whirlpool Rapids in a barrel, the same barrel used the next day by Maude Willard. The year 1901 was about to become the "year of the lady stunters at Niagara Falls."

Twenty

On August 6, 1901, Joe Chambers became one of a handful of men to successfully swim through the Whirlpool Rapids.

Twenty-One

In the afternoon of Monday, July 9, 1900, Peter M. Nissen, alias P. M. Bowser, 31, from Chicago, rode a 20-foot-long boat he called the "Fool Killer" through the Whirlpool Rapids. After circling the Whirlpool four times, he was rescued by a group of men who towed his boat to the shore. Nissen was uninjured but quite cold, shivering uncontrollably.

"It was an awful experience," he told reporters, adding, "the Whirlpool Rapids are nothing at all like what I had thought they were. They are many times rougher. I have no idea of trying the trick again."

Well, he changed his mind. On Saturday afternoon, October 12, 1901, he repeated his stunt in a larger steam powered boat, "Fool Killer No. 2." This time he said the ride was more pleasant, even though the boat was badly damaged.

He kept the boat moored on the shore of the Whirlpool. On the morning of October 18, he discovered the boat missing. It had some-how broken its moorings and drifted downriver, or so he thought. It was never found — not even a trace of it. Perhaps it sank in the Whirlpool? This was to become one of Niagara's many mysteries.

One of the things Nissen did while Fool Killer No. 2 was in the Whirlpool was take soundings along the shore. He said the average depth was only 35 feet and the bottom was all sand. He made a wild speculation that there might be gold in the sand. (No one has ever found gold by the Whirlpool.)

Twenty-Two

On July 1, 1896, James E. Hardy, 26, became the youngest person to cross the gorge on a tightrope. He made sixteen crossings.

Twenty-Three

In the afternoon of Wednesday, June 22, 1887, Stephen Peere, 47, walked on the thinnest cable ever stretched across the gorge. Three days later, he and two companions went out to the platform from which he started his stunt. It was evening and the men had apparently been drinking. While his companions were distracted by something, Peere went out and began to walk on his cable. Without a sound, he fell forty-five feet to his death. He was the only Niagara funambulist to die from a fall into the gorge.

Twenty-Four

On November 28, 1886, George Hazlett and his girlfriend, Sadie Allen, went on a most unusual date. They rode a barrel through the Whirlpool Rapids. They survived.

Twenty-Five

On August 22, 1886, William J. Kendall, a Boston, Massachusetts, policeman, swam through the Whirlpool Rapids wearing only his trunks and a cork life preserver. He suffered only minor injuries.

Above Photo From: Niagara Falls, NY Public Library

*William Kendall, the Boston policeman who swam through
the Whirlpool Rapids. Notice his cork life preserver*

Twenty-Six

At about 11 A.M., on Saturday, December 11, 1886, "Professor" Alphonse King, a 31-year-old Frenchman, made an attempt to "walk" on the river below the falls. He had made a wager with a few men that he could "walk" one hundred feet on the water.

King came prepared with a strange set of tin shoes which he called "Gold Fish." Each shoe was 32 inches long, 8 inches wide, and 9 inches deep. The upper part resembled a fish, with its tail and head turned up. The bottom was flat with automatic paddles carefully attached.

When the "Professor" approached the swirling currents at the center of the river, he lost his footing and fell flat on his face. Lucky for him, men in a nearby boat pulled him out before he drowned.

Determined to not just walk 100 feet but actually cross the river, King set out again. This time he fell on his back. Once again he had to be rescued. Soaked, tired, and probably feeling embarrassed, he gave up.

The next year, on August 16 at about 4:42 P.M., he returned and did something almost as strange as his first stunt. Using a contraption he called a "Water Bicycle," he pedaled all over the lower river with relative ease. He made one crossing in 4.5 minutes.

Twenty-Seven

At about noon, on Sunday, June 8, 1888, a white bantam rooster went over the Horseshoe Falls in the same barrel George Hazlett and William Potts had used to ride through the Whirlpool Rapids on August 8, 1886. After the poor bird failed to survive the plunge, neither Hazlett or Potts desired to follow through with the plan for one of them to ride the same barrel over the falls.

Twenty-Eight

In the afternoon of Sunday, July 11, 1886, Carlisle D. Graham, from Philadelphia, successfully rode an oak barrel through the Whirlpool Rapids. This was the first barrel stunt at Niagara Falls. The trip made him ill and dizzy, but he repeated it three more times. On his second trip, he held his head out of the barrel. That experience made him hard of hearing the rest of his life. He must have been a glutton for punishment.

Twenty-Nine

As far as it is known, the first person to swim across the English Channel was Captain Matthew Webb, who accomplished the feat on August 24 and 25, 1875.

At 4:25 P.M., on Tuesday, July 24, 1883, Webb attempted to swim through the Whirlpool Rapids. He wore the same pair of red cotton swimming trunks he wore when he swam across the English Channel, perhaps for good luck. Things went well at first, but when he was hit by a giant wave, he cried out for help and went under for about 150 feet before reappearing, unconscious. Then his body disappeared and was not found until four days later, between Lewiston and Youngstown.

Thirty

During the first week of July, 1876, as part of the local celebration of the United States Centennial, Maria Spelterina, 23, became the only female tightrope walker to perform at Niagara Falls. She did just about every stunt done by her male predecessors. She did not carry anyone on her back, however.

She crossed more than once wearing snug-fitting peach baskets. She even crossed with her arms and legs shackled in chains. She is especially remembered for her unusual costume and hat.

Thirty-One

On Monday, August 25, 1873, Henry Bellini, from Australia, began semiweekly performances on a 1,500-foot long rope across the gorge — the longest rope ever used at Niagara Falls. During the first three performances, Bellini jumped 160 feet in to the lower river, restrained each time by a rubber cord. On the third jump, the cord broke and wound itself around Bellini's feet. With his feet still not free, Bellini struggled to the surface. He was rescued by men in a small boat. Terrified by his near drowning, he decided he would never jump again.

Thirty-Two

On August 15, 1860, William T. Hunt, alias "Signor Farini," walked a tightrope across the gorge. One of his notable stunts involved a washing machine. He carried it on his back to the center of the rope. After setting the machine down, he lowered a pail to the river, drew up water and washed the handkerchief of a lady on board the Maid of the Mist boat.

Thirty-Three

Sometime in 1860, Joel Robinson, a local riverman and hero, walked through the American Rapids from Prospect Point to an island northeast of Luna Island. Using an iron staff, he calmly returned to the mainland. The island he visited was later named after him.

Thirty-Four

During the summer of 1859, Niagara's first and greatest funambulist, Jean Francois Gravelet, alias "The Great Blondin," a 35-year-old Frenchman, made 21 very popular crossings on a 1,100-foot long rope stretched from Prospect Park to the Canadian side. He originally wanted to place the rope closer to the falls, but the owners of the property would not allow it.

On August 17, Blondin carried his agent, Henry Colcord, across the gorge on his back. The trip lasted 42 minutes, including seven rest stops in which Colcord dismounted and stood on the rope, totally at the mercy of Blondin's abilities.

Above Photo From: Niagara Falls, NY Public Library

Blondin crossing gorge with his manager on his back.

Having enjoyed so much success, Blondin returned in 1860 and made several more appearances on the same rope he used the year before. Before one of his performances, he offered to carry the Prince of Wales (later King Edward VII) on his back. (The prince was touring Canada at that time.) The prince politely refused.

Blondin returned to Europe and renewed performing after a short retirement. He ended up settling in England, naming his estate "Niagara."

Many people tried to imitate Blondin's stunts, including children. In July of 1859, a Cincinnati, Ohio, girl, trying to do a "Niagara feat," fell to her death from the second floor porch railing of her parents' house.

Thirty-Five

On October 17, 1829, the first of Niagara's many daredevils, Sam Patch, a 22-year-old from Rhode Island, jumped off a platform at the top of a 98-foot high ladder set up below Goat Island, not far from the Cave of the Winds. It was a miserable day, with rain pouring in torrents. Even so, a huge crowd was on hand to witness Patch's stunt.

After Patch entered the water, it seemed like an eternity before his head bobbed up from the turbulent water. As he swam to the shore, the crowd cheered loudly.

Enthused by his success at Niagara Falls, Patch decided to jump by the Genesee Falls in Rochester, New York. For some reason, he was not true to form when he made his leap on November 6, 1829. Instead of diving headfirst, he landed on his side. It proved to be a fatal mistake.

Heroic Acts and Accidents

Thirty-Six

At 12:18 P.M., on Tuesday, September 29, 1992, two sight-seeing helicopters collided in the misty skies over the Horseshoe Falls. One, an American helicopter, crashed at the foot of the Niagara Parks Incline Railway, just below the Minolta Tower, killing the pilot and his three passengers. The other, a Canadian helicopter, despite serious damage, was able to safely land in the parking lot at Marineland. Its pilot suffered a shoulder injury. His four passengers were shaken up but uninjured.

After a lengthy investigation by American and Canadian authorities, it was suggested that the crash was due to human error.

The first fatal sight-seeing helicopter accident by the falls took place on Tuesday, August 5, 1969. An American copter crashed into the Canadian Rapids, killing its pilot and two passengers. This accident was caused by mechanical failure.

Thirty-Seven

On the sunny afternoon of Saturday, July 9, 1960, James Honeycutt, 40, took Deane Woodward, 17, and her brother, Roger, 7, for a ride in his 14-foot aluminum boat. Honeycutt was a friend of the children's father, who along with his wife, didn't feel like joining their children for the ride. Lucky for them.

The boat ride began a few miles above the falls where the Niagara River is frequented by all kinds of boats. Thinking they might go for a swim, the Woodward children wore only their bathing suits. Little did they anticipate that their entrance into the water would become a part of what has been often called "The Miracle at Niagara Falls."

Honeycutt decided to give the children a real "thrill" by taking them close to the Canadian Rapids, beyond the "point of no return" where the river's character changes very quickly from friend to foe. Realizing his mistake, Honeycutt tried desperately to head the boat and his terrified passengers to Goat Island, but the boat's motor was disabled by rocks.

Above Photo From: Maid of the Mist Steamboat Co.

Roger Woodward about to be rescued by Jack Hopkins,
a deck hand of the maid of the mist boat.

Honeycutt paddled frantically but the much stronger current took control of the craft, somersaulting it in the misty air and tossing him and Roger ahead. The boat landed on Deane but she was able to struggle free. She was not able to maintain a grip on the boat. She and her companions were now at the mercy of the rapids.

Only the children wore life jackets. Being a strong swimmer, Deane was able to get close to the shore of Goat Island by Terrapin Point. John R. Hayes and John Quattrochi, tourists from New Jersey, risked their lives to pull Deane out of the water. Working as a team, each man got hold of one of the girl's hands. The rescue took place a mere fifteen feet from the brink of the waterfall.

Meanwhile, Roger and Jim Honeycutt held on to each other until a strong current separated them near the falls. They both went over at the same time falling about 170 feet.

Moments later, Roger was spotted in the water just below the falls by Clifford Keech, the captain of one of the Maid of the Mist boats. Keech and his passengers couldn't believe their eyes. Very carefully the boat approached the boy and tossed him a life saver. After he was pulled onto the deck, everyone was surprised to see that the boy had only minor injuries. He kept asking about his sister.

How did Roger survive what should have been a fatal plunge? First of all, he was small. Second, he probably landed on a water cone, a mass of water forced up by compressed air. Third, he missed landing on the rocks scattered about the bottom of the flank of the Horseshoe Fall.

Honeycutt's body was recovered four days later. No one expected him to survive.

Thirty-Eight

On July 18, 1933, William Kondrat was walking at the bottom of the gorge. Before he knew what happened, he slipped and fell into the Whirlpool Rapids. He kept trying to get back to the rocky shore but the 39 miles-per-hour current swept him along. Somehow, relatively unscathed, he made it to the Whirlpool where he was rescued.

Thirty-Nine

In 1886, the feasibility of constructing a railroad at the bottom of the American side of the Niagara River gorge was seriously questioned by many people. The Buffalo Express, for example, discussed the dangers from falling rocks and debris "along this shaly, shaky slope."

In spite of the warnings, after five years of arduous work, the Great Gorge Route electric railway opened on July 15, 1895. The trolley cars, some with open sides, took people from downtown Niagara Falls, New York, into the gorge, all the way to the village of Lewiston.

Starting in 1899, the Great Gorge Route was connected to the Canadian belt line. Trolley cars went over the new Lewiston-Queenston Suspension Bridge, up the Niagara Escarpment and along the top of the

THE NIAGARA GORGE BELT LINE
"THE GREAT GORGE ROUTE"

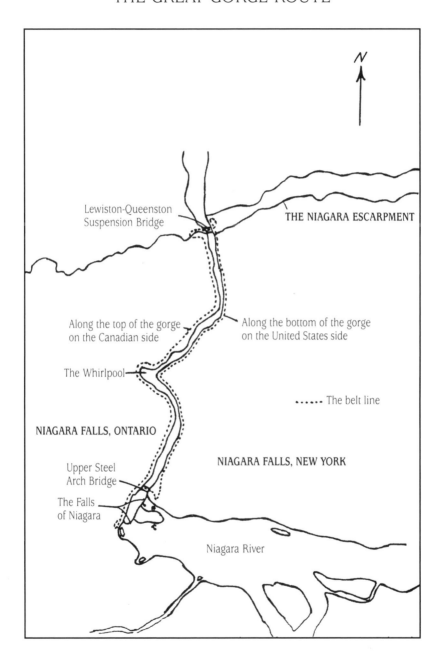

N

Lewiston-Queenston
Suspension Bridge

THE NIAGARA ESCARPMENT

Along the top of the gorge
on the Canadian side

Along the bottom of the gorge
on the United States side

The Whirlpool

•••••• The belt line

NIAGARA FALLS, ONTARIO

NIAGARA FALLS, NEW YORK

Upper Steel
Arch Bridge

The Falls
of Niagara

Niagara River

Canadian side of the gorge to Queen Victoria Park. From there, the cars turned back and went over the Falls View Bridge and back to downtown Niagara Falls, New York.

The route became very popular with both local people and tourists. At its peak, as many as 300,000 passengers were carried each season.

Just as predicted years before, falling rocks and debris were a constant problem and expense. Surprisingly, during its 40 years of operation, not one passenger was directly injured by falling rocks. There was an incident, however, involving falling debris. In 1913, an open car was passing under the old Niagara Falls garbage disposal plant. Just at the right moment, a garbage chute broke, sending a smelly mass of wastes onto and into the trolley. There were no fatalities. Some people were injured. All of the passengers were quite embarrassed and unhappy.

There were a few serious accidents involving the trolley cars and their tracks. In 1910, after a collision, one car went down an embankment and into the rapids. Twelve people were killed.

In July of 1917, heavy rains caused a section of the roadbed to give way, sending about 60 people into the river. The death count was never accurately determined because the fare register was lost — another of Niagara's mysteries.

In the fall of 1935, a huge landslide of shale buried a large section of track in the gorge. This convinced the owners of the railway that they could no longer afford its upkeep. The Great Gorge Route closed.

Forty

On the hot and muggy afternoon of August 6, 1918, James Harris, 53, and Gustave Lofberg, 51, crewmen on a scow being towed in the upper Niagara River, suddenly found themselves at the mercy of the river's dangerous currents. The tug boat towing the scow became grounded in a sand bar. When it was freed, the line between it and the scow broke. Two other tugs gave chase, but they were not able to get a line to the scow.

Desperate, Harris and Lofberg opened their craft's dumping doors. Water came rushing in. The scow settled in a shallow part of the Canadian Rapids, about 2,500 feet above the brink of the Horseshoe Fall, and about 1,000 feet from the Toronto Powerhouse.

The rest of that day, Canadian and American rescuers worked together feverishly to get lines to the stranded men, but the lines kept getting tangled. It wasn't until the next morning that the Canadian riverman and war hero, William "Red" Hill Sr., was able to untangle the lines and get a breeches buoy to the scow. One by one, first Harris, then Lofberg, the exhausted crewmen were carried to the roof of the powerhouse.

The scow has been lying in the rapids ever since, slowly rusting and breaking up. It has become a significant part of the human history at Niagara Falls.

Forty-One

Around noon, on Sunday, February 4, 1912, there were only about 25 people on the ice bridge below the falls. It was bitterly cold, but the popular ice formation would become crowded with people later in the afternoon, as was the custom in those days. Most of them came to the falls on excursion trains.

Among the group on the ice that day were a couple from Toronto, Mr. and Mrs. Eldridge Stanton, and two men from Cleveland, Ignatius Roth, a wealthy businessman, and Burrel Heacock, a young man out for an adventure. Also on the ice was "Red" Hill Sr., the local man who would later become famous for rescuing the two men from the scow stranded in the Canadian Rapids.

Without any warning, a rumbling sound was almost instantly followed by a breaking up of the ice bridge. Hill shouted for everyone to head for the shores. Everyone, except for Roth, Heacock and the Stantons, escaped. Hill was able to pull Roth off a floe. Heacock could have made it, too, but he turned back to assist the Stantons, who, he must have assumed, needed help.

It wasn't long before the floe with its three passengers started moving downriver to the Whirlpool Rapids. Frantic efforts were made to rescue them. Before it approached the two bridges over the Whirlpool

Rapids, the floe broke into two pieces — Heacock on one, the Stantons on the other. Ropes were sent down from the bridges, but efforts by the doomed trio to secure themselves proved futile. Soon they were thrown into the water, never to be seen again.

Since that tragic incident, people have not been permitted to go on the ice bridges. An era had ended.

Falling Water and Falling Rocks

Prospect Point at the moment it began to fall. Similar rockfalls have helped to create the Niagara River gorge.

Forty-Two

In June of 1954, large amounts of groundwater were seen flowing through cracks in the shaft walls of an abandoned elevator just below the American Falls. On the morning of Wednesday, July 28, large cracks appeared in the asphalt at Prospect Point, one of the favorite spots from which to view the falls and gorge. Authorities quickly roped off the point. They expected a terrible fall of rock.

At 4:50 that afternoon, it happened — the largest rockfall ever recorded at Niagara Falls. The section which fell was about 360 feet long and 130 feet wide, and it weighed about 185,000 tons. It made a significant addition to the talus (fallen rocks) which had been accumulating below the American and Bridal Veil Falls for hundreds of years.

That same year, on December 4, about 15,000 tons of rock fell from the crest of the American Falls, not far from Luna Island. The rockmass measured about 190 feet long and 40 feet wide.

The second largest rockfall at Niagara Falls took place at about 5:40 P.M., on Saturday, January 17, 1931, at the American Falls, about 300 feet from Luna Island. The section which fell was about 280 feet long and 70 feet wide, and it weighed about 76,000 tons. The talus piled up quite high, making the free fall of the water about one third of what it could be.

After the area around Prospect Point was made safe, it was reopened to the public on November 13, 1954. Since then, all observations points near the three Niagara Falls have been made secure.

Forty-Three

Table Rock is a very popular observation area in Canada at the top of the gorge, just north of the flank of the Horseshoe Falls. Hundreds of years ago, it was a very different place. In fact, a part of the upper Niagara River flowed there and formed a beautiful shoot of water from a 58-foot projection of hard rock. As the years passed, the Horseshoe receded and the river stopped flowing over the projection.

The passage of time also gave the elements and the processes of erosion a chance to gradually diminish the size of Table Rock. Large pieces broke off in 1818, 1823, 1829, 1846, 1850 and 1853. Even so, this location became the favorite place from which to view the falls.

The most outstanding human event to happen at Table Rock took place in 1857, when Frederick Edwin Church, an artist from New York State, sat there and created Niagara, the most famous painting of the Horseshoe Falls.

In 1935, what was left of Table Rock was blasted away. This was done to make the area below safer.

Above Photo From: Houghton Library, Harvard University

Table Rock as it appeared in 1837.

Forty-Four

The year 1816 is known in the Niagara region as "the year without a summer," because there were frosts in June, July, August and September. In May of that year, so much ice from Lake Erie accumulated above the falls that the American and Bridal Veil Falls were just about turned off. It was possible to go to the islands in the upper rapids just by walking on the ice. (There were no bridges to any of the islands at that time.)

(Accumulations of ice both above and below the falls have always been an integral part of the process of recession of the falls. The ice breaks up rocks and erodes the gorge and river shores.)

That May, Parkhurst Whitney, a businessman from the village of Manchester (now part of the city of Niagara Falls, New York) took his three young daughters to visit the islands above the falls. The girls especially liked exploring four picturesque little islands south of Goat Island.

Whitney thought it would be nice to name those little islands after his daughters and infant son. He approached the owners of the islands, Peter and Augustus Porter, with the idea, and they agreed to it. What were once known as the Moss Islands became the Three Sisters Islands (Asenath, Angeline and Celinda Eliza) and Little Brother Island (Solon).

It's interesting to note that all the islands above Niagara Falls were created when the height of the Horseshoe Falls began to decrease a few thousand years ago, dropping the depth of Lake Erie and the upper Niagara River.

Forty-Five

About 12,500 years ago, at the end of the Ice Age, there was only one waterfall in the Niagara River. It poured directly into a much deeper Lake Ontario just below the Niagara Escarpment, over seven miles north of the three Niagara Falls of today. That original falls, now known as the Horseshoe or Canadian Falls, receded south at a rate of one to seven feet per year, depending upon the amount of water coming from Lake Erie. Sometimes, Lake Erie did not receive the waters from all three of the other four upper Great Lakes. When that happened, the Horseshoe Falls had less erosive power and receded more slowly. At those times, the gorge was made narrow and shallow.

A few times, as the falls receded, streams which had previously emptied into the upper Niagara River produced small waterfalls which eventually dried up (the Niagara Glen) or shrank to a trickle (Devil's Hole and Smeaton Ravine).

About 700 years ago, the Horseshoe Falls separated from the American and Bridal Veil Falls by Luna Island. Since more than ninety percent of the upper Niagara River goes into the Canadian Rapids and over the Horseshoe Falls, that waterfall will continue to be the creator of the beautiful gorge. The American and Bridal Veil Falls have much less water and erosive power, so they will never produce their own gorge. Instead, they will eventually become a steep rapid until the time when the Horseshoe Falls passes Goat Island. Then the upper river will send all of its water to the Horseshoe Falls, drying up the American and Bridal Veil Falls. That will happen thousands of years from now. Not to worry.

The Maid
of the
Mist Boats

The second Maid of the Mist boat passing through the Whirlpool Rapids on June 15, 1861. Its smokestack was lost during the treacherous journey. Its captain, Joel Robinson, was a local riverman and daredevil.

Forty-Six

On June 13, 1885, for the first time since 1861, a Maid of the Mist steamer again sailed below the falls and took people for a breathtaking ride right up to the Horseshoe Falls. The 70-foot long boat was made of the finest white oak. On July 14, 1892, a second Maid of the Mist boat was launched. The 83-foot long boat was also made of white oak.

(It is interesting to note that huge white oak trees once thrived in the forests around the falls.)

Forty-Seven

In the afternoon of June 15, 1861, Joel Robinson, with the able assistance of two crewmen, piloted the recently sold Maid of the Mist boat through all the lower rapids to Queenston, Ontario. Robinson survived the trip, but it changed him for the rest of his life. He became much less adventurous .

Here is Mark Twain's account of Robinson's ride, after it was related to him by a local tour guide during his visit to the falls in 1869.

"The guide will explain to you, in his blood-curdling way, how he saw the little steamer, Maid of the Mist, descend the fearful rapids — how first one paddle-box was out of sight behind raging billows, and then the other, and at what point it was that her smokestack toppled overboard, and where her planking began to break and part asunder — and how she did finally live through the trip, after accomplishing the incredible feat of travelling seventeen miles in six minutes, or six miles in seventeen minutes, I have really forgotten which. But it was very extraordinary, anyhow. It is worth the price of admission to hear the guide tell the story nine times in succession to different parties, and never miss a word or alter a sentence or a gesture."

Forty-Eight

The first Maid of the Mist boat was launched in 1846. The name for that boat (and all future "Maids") came from the ancient Native American legend. The boat was never really a great success. It was replaced by a second boat in 1854, and this boat was larger and more successful, at least for awhile. The second boat was the one Joel Robinson piloted to Queenston.

Turning Off the Falls

The Mighty Torrent . . .

Turns To A Trickle

Photograph given to me by Chuck Steiner, President, Niagara Area Chamber of Commerce
The dewatered American and Bridal Veil Falls

Forty-Nine

From June 12 to November 26 of 1969, the American and Bridal Veil Falls were almost completely turned off by the United States Army Corps of Engineers. The project was accomplished by the construction of an earth and stone cofferdam from the mainland to the head of Goat Island.

There were three main reasons for the dewatering. First, to determine if the erosion of the falls could or should be controlled. Second, to determine if the removal of talus from the base of the falls was desirable and possible. Third, to determine if other measures were needed to preserve the beauty of the falls.

During the project, water was sprinkled on the bed of the American Rapids to keep the hot summer sunlight from expanding the numerous cracks in the rock. The vegetation on the islands and islets scattered throughout the rapids was also watered.

Most people who witnessed the undertaking were intrigued and surprised. Some were disappointed to see the falls in an unnatural condition.

There were six major results of the study of the dewatered falls. First, it was decided that the overall guiding policy for the future of the falls should involve an acceptance of the process of change as a powerful part of the natural conditions of the falls. Second, the processes of erosion and recession should not be interrupted. Third, removal of the talus from the base of the falls would be too costly. Fourth, the recession of the falls should be allowed to continue because of the costs to stop it, and because to do so would make the falls even more artificial than they already are. Fifth, other ways of artificially "improving" the appearance of the falls, such as raising the water level in the lower river or by diverting more water to the American and Bridal Veil Falls, were found to be possible but not desirable. Sixth, measures should be implemented to make all viewing areas safer.

Fifty

The winter of 1847-48 had been unusually cold around the Great Lakes. Lake Erie was covered from shore to shore with a three-foot thick layer of ice. Late in March, after a prolonged warm spell, strong winds broke the lake ice up into countless floes.

During the daylight hours of March 29, a powerful east wind drove most of the floes to the western end of the lake. Later in the day, around sunset, an even stronger gale from the southwest moved the ice east to the source of the Niagara River, at Buffalo. It wasn't long before a monstrous ice dam formed, preventing the lake waters from taking their normal path to the north. Slowly, silently, while the people on both sides of the river slept, the mighty river shrank into a few small streams surrounded by numerous grounded ice floes.

Just past midnight, the American and Bridal Veil Falls became completely dry, while the Horseshoe Falls was reduced to a small waterfall at its center. The thunder was silenced; the mist vanished.

All during the daylight hours of March 30, many people explored the riverbed, gathering fish and looking for mementoes. The phenomenon excited most people, while a few had fears about it. That evening, with a mighty roar, the ice dam at Buffalo broke, sending ice floes and lake water rushing to the falls.

Never before, as far as it is known, and never since has nature turned off the falls.

The Native Americans, The People Who Called the River "The Neck"

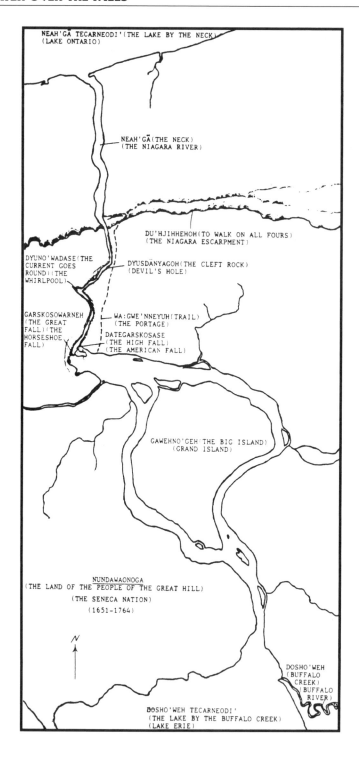

Fifty-One

In 1764, as retribution for attacking British soldiers and settlers the previous year during Pontiac's Rebellion (an uprising of the Great Lakes Native American people led by a man named Pontiac), the Six Nations or Iroquois Confederation were forced to give the British the lands on both sides of the Niagara River, from Lake Erie to Lake Ontario. The Seneca Nation, the Iroquois who occupied those lands, were still permitted to travel through and hunt there.

There are Senecas living today who argue that the treaties made later with the government of the United States were never properly ratified, especially regarding the islands in the Niagara River. It will probably take the courts a long time to resolve this situation.

Fifty-Two

On September 14, 1763, as a part of Pontiac's Rebellion, a group of young dissident Seneca men, angry with the British for no longer paying them to assist with the operation of the portage around the gorge and falls, ambushed a wagon train just above the Devil's Hole, a cleft in the gorge near present-day Niagara University.

The Senecas slaughtered more than a dozen men, throwing their bodies, their wagons, and their horses into the steep ravine. Only two people survived the attack. One was John Stedman, the wagonmaster. He was able to get away on his horse, despite numerous attempts to kill him. The other survivor was a drummer boy, who threw himself over the cliff and was lucky when his suspenders got caught in the branches of a tree.

The small British garrison at Fort Gray, located north of Devil's Hole at the top of the Niagara Escarpment, heard the fracas and hurried to assist the wagon train. They were all killed.

Fifty-Three

Two important Native American legends involve Niagara Falls. No one is certain whether these legends were created by the Iroquois or the people before them.

Both legends have as their main character, Heno, the Thunder Being, who supposedly lived in a huge grotto behind the Great Falls (Horseshoe or Canadian Falls). Heno was responsible for the health of the people and the success of their crops. He also protected the people from a giant evil serpent which lived in the Niagara River gorge. Heno's struggles with the serpent often caused rocks to fall. At one encounter, the fighting was so furious that the middle of the Great Falls was knocked down, destroying much of Heno's grotto and creating the horseshoe-shaped crestline.

The second legend is about a young woman who decided to take her life by going over the Great Falls in her white canoe. She was quite unhappy because she was being forced to marry someone she didn't love. Just as the canoe went over the brink, Heno caught it and took it and the woman into his grotto. There he comforted her and restored her will to live. Then he sent her back to her village, where she surprised everyone with her wisdom and patience — gifts from Heno.

The Tug-of-War Along the River Niagara's Colonial History

Above Photo: Ron Paré

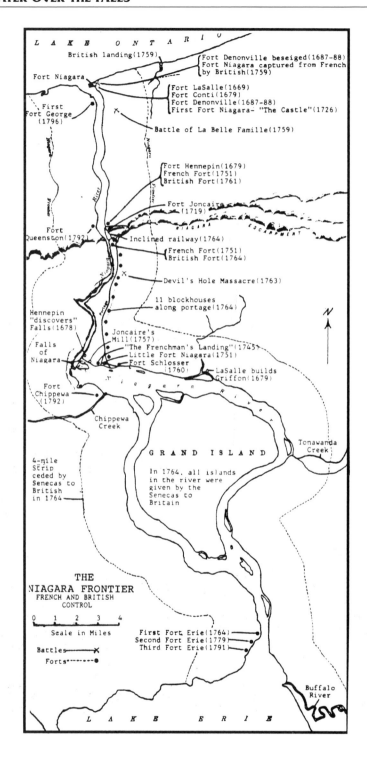

L A K E   O N T A R I O

British landing(1759)

Fort Niagara

Fort Denonville beseiged(1687-88)
Fort Niagara captured from French
by British(1759)

First
Fort George
(1796)

Fort LaSalle(1669)
Fort Conti(1679)
Fort Denonville(1687-88)
First Fort Niagara- "The Castle"(1726)

Battle of La Belle Famille(1759)

Fort Hennepin(1679)
French Fort(1751)
British Fort(1761)

Fort Joncaire
(1719)

N I A G A R A   E S C A R P M E N T

Fort
Queenston(1792)

Inclined railway(1764)

French Fort(1751)
British Fort(1764)

Devil's Hole Massacre(1763)

11 blockhouses
along portage(1764)

Hennepin
"discovers"
Falls(1678)

Joncaire's
Mill(1757)

Falls
of
Niagara

"The Frenchman's Landing"(1745)
Little Fort Niagara(1751)
Fort Schlosser
(1760)

LaSalle builds
Griffon(1679)

Fort
Chippewa
(1792)

N i a g a r a   R i v e r

Chippewa
Creek

Tonawanda
Creek

G R A N D   I S L A N D

4-mile
Strip
ceded by
Senecas to
British
in 1764

In 1764, all islands
in the river were
given by the
Senecas to
Britain

N

THE
NIAGARA FRONTIER
FRENCH AND BRITISH
CONTROL

0   1   2   3   4

Scale in Miles

Battles ———×
Forts ------●

First Fort Erie(1764)
Second Fort Erie(1779)
Third Fort Erie(1791)

Buffalo
River

L A K E   E R I E

𝓕𝓲𝓯𝓽𝔂-𝓕𝓸𝓾𝓻

In 1794, African-American slaves from the United States began their flight across the Niagara River to freedom in Canada. This was made possible by the passage of the Canadian Fugitive Slave Act of 1793, which allowed slaves to seek asylum in Canada. Risking their lives, the fleeing slaves crossed the river at places such at Broderick's Point in Buffalo and the Tyron house in Lewiston. Some crossed over the ice on Lake Erie.

𝓕𝓲𝓯𝓽𝔂-𝓕𝓲𝓿𝓮

When the American Revolution began in 1775, Fort Niagara became a refuge for British loyalists and Native American allies who lost their homes and land to the Americans. At the fort, Colonel John Butler organized a corps of farmers and merchants who had lost their properties in the Mohawk Valley of New York. Along with Sir William Johnson's "Royal Green" and Joseph Brant's Mohawks, Butlers "Rangers" used the fort as a base from which they often raided American outposts and settlements in New York and Pennsylvania. The rangers created a reign of terror wherever they went.

𝓕𝓲𝓯𝓽𝔂-𝓢𝓲𝔁

In 1760, the British constructed Fort Schlosser on the site of the French Little Fort Niagara. As its predecessor, Fort Schlosser controlled the upper end of the Niagara portage road, the most important route for sending goods and troops to the western outposts.

From 1760 to 1796 (the British did not give up control of the United States side of the Niagara River until 1796), John Stedman, one of the two survivors of the Devil's Hole Massacre, was in charge of the portage. He built a large house around a chimney which was once a part of a French dwelling. Today, that chimney, moved twice, stands downriver close to the original end of the Niagara portage.

Fifty-Seven

On July 24, 1759, a force of about 600 French troops and 1,500 Native American allies hurriedly came from western outposts in an attempt to raise the British siege of Fort Niagara. British colonials and their Iroquois allies, led by Sir William Johnson, the flamboyant commissioner of Native American affairs for the British crown, ambushed the French reinforcements at a beautiful place along the lower Niagara River called La Belle Famille ("The Beautiful Family"), about two miles south of Fort Niagara. The French and their allies suffered a terrible defeat.

The following day, Captain Pierre Pouchot, commandant of Fort Niagara, realizing he had no chance of repelling the British forces, surrendered. That action ended French control of the Niagara region and its strategic portage.

Fifty-Eight

In 1757, Chabert Joncaire, a French trader and friend of the Iroquois, cut a narrow loop canal into the bank of the river at the head of the American Rapids, just east of the present American Rapids Bridge. Using a wooden overshot wheel (a wheel driven by water flowing onto the upper part), under a head of about six feet, he generated water power to cut logs. This mill was the first structure built close to the falls and the first application of the river's power for manufacturing something.

In 1759, the French burnt down the mill when they realized that the British were about to defeat them. The British rebuilt the mill in 1760. They used it for years to produce lumber.

When the property by the falls was purchased by Peter and Augustus Porter in the early 1800's, they enlarged the mill. By the middle of the nineteenth century, many other mills were located above the American Fall. All of the mills were torn down when the Niagara Reservation opened in the 1800's.

Above Photo From: Old Fort Niagara Association

The Castle at Old Fort Niagara, built in 1726.

Fifty-Nine

In 1726, the French constructed the "House of Peace," known today as "The Castle." It was placed right at the mouth of the Niagara River, and it was destined to become the most important part of Old Fort Niagara, which was expanded and changed many times by the French, the British and the Americans. The castle has usually served primarily as officers' quarters. Today, it appears much as it did when first constructed.

A visit to Niagara Falls is not complete without a visit to Old Fort Niagara. The drive to the fort along the lower Niagara River is quite scenic and relaxing. Outside the old fort is Fort Niagara State Park, a wonderful place to "get away from it all" and enjoy the out-of-doors either by the river or the shore of Lake Ontario.

Sixty

In 1721, Father Charlevoix, a French Roman Catholic missionary, was the first visitor to give an accurate estimate of the heights of the falls. He was also the first person to describe the Canadian Falls as having a "horseshoe shape."

Sixty-One

The French explorer, Robert LaSalle, built Fort Conti in 1679, the first fort on the site of Old Fort Niagara. That year, he also built the Griffon, the first ship to sail the upper Great Lakes. The ship was made by an island along the shore of the upper Niagara River, a few miles above the falls. The area around that island is now a part of the city of Niagara Falls, New York, called LaSalle.

Fort Conti accidentally burnt down the same year it was built, and the French didn't replace it with another fort until 1687, when Fort Denonville was erected. That fort was abandoned in the spring of 1688, after most of the garrison died from disease or were killed by hostile Iroquois warriors. At that time, tensions between the French and the Iroquois were high because of earlier French incursions into Iroquois villages.

Sixty-Two

When LaSalle came to the Niagara region in 1678, he was accompanied by a number of other men, including a Roman Catholic priest, Father Louis Hennepin. Hennepin's job was to see to the spiritual needs of LaSalle and his assistants and to attempt to convert the Native Americans encountered.

The Senecas told Hennepin about the mighty falls and how they sometimes saw the Creator in the mist. Curiosity and a chance to perform his duties moved Hennepin to insist on being escorted to the falls. Despite the snowy December weather, a group of Senecas took him to the natural wonder. He called the Niagara Escarpment "The Three Mountains," as he huffed and puffed his way up the three steep inclines. The Senecas had their own name for the place-"Crawl-on-all-fours."

After trudging through the snow along the portage, Hennepin finally beheld the great torrents on either side of an island. He was so taken with the sight that he took his portable wooden altar off his back and said a mass. According to tradition, the spot from which he first saw the falls is just north of the present-day American Prospect Point Observation Tower. There is a stone marker on that spot.

Even though he probably wasn't, Hennepin is said to have been the first foreigner to see Niagara Falls. When he returned to Europe, years later, he wrote about his visit to Niagara Falls. He also had an artist make a rendering of his recollections of the falls.

Above Photo From: Niagara Falls, NY Public Library

Father Hennepin's depiction of Niagara Falls made in 1697.

The War of
1812

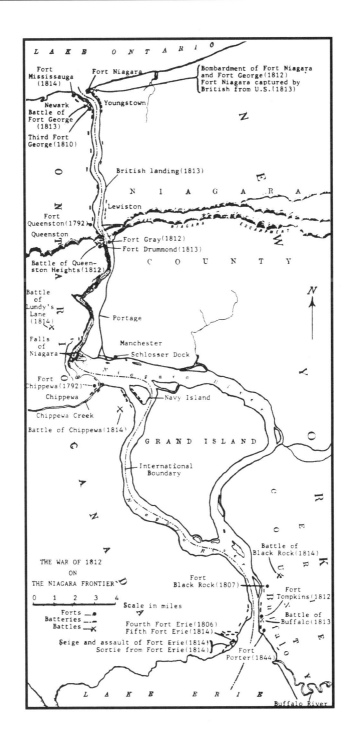

LAKE ONTARIO

Fort
Mississauga
(1814)

Fort Niagara

Bombardment of Fort Niagara
and Fort George (1812)
Fort Niagara captured by
British from U.S. (1813)

Youngstown

Newark
Battle of
Fort George
(1813)

Third Fort
George (1810)

British landing (1813)

NIAGARA

Lewiston

Fort
Queenston (1792)

Queenston

Fort Gray (1812)
Fort Drummond (1813)

NIAGARA ESCARPMENT

Battle of Queen-
ston Heights (1812)

COUNTY

Battle
of
Lundy's
Lane
(1814)

Portage

Falls
of
Niagara

Manchester
Schlosser Dock

Fort
Chippewa (1792)

Niagara River

Chippewa

Navy Island

Chippewa Creek

Battle of Chippewa (1814)

GRAND ISLAND

International
Boundary

Niagara River

Battle of
Black Rock (1814)

THE WAR OF 1812
ON
THE NIAGARA FRONTIER

Fort
Black Rock (1807)

Fort
Tompkins (1812)

Battle of
Buffalo (1813)

0   1   2   3   4
Scale in miles

Forts
Batteries
Battles

Fourth Fort Erie (1806)
Fifth Fort Erie (1814)

Seige and assault of Fort Erie (1814)
Sortie from Fort Erie (1814)

Fort
Porter (1844)

Buffalo River

LAKE   ERIE

Sixty-Three

In 1819, the Boundary Commissioners for Canada and the United States, under the terms of the Treaty of Ghent, confirmed the original International Boundary Line along the Niagara River established by Jay's Treaty of 1794. Since that time, except for a few minor incidents, peace had prevailed along the border.

Sixty-Four

On December 24, 1814, the Treaty of Ghent, known to many as the "Peace of Christmas Eve," ended the War of 1812. War with Britain had been declared by the United States on June 18, 1812. Britain did not declare war until January 9, 1813. The reasons for the unpopular war have been debated ever since it ended.

Sixty-Five

Over eighty percent of the land battles of the War of 1812 in North America took place along the Niagara River, mostly on the Canadian side. The bloodiest battle took place at Lundy's Lane (now in the city of Niagara Falls, Ontario) on July 25, 1814. The result of the night-long conflict was a stalemate. The flashes of light from the incessant firing of the artillery lit up the distant falls.

About three weeks earlier, on July 5, another great battle had taken place at Chippewa, Ontario. American forces, led by Brigadier General Winfield Scott, defeated the British and Canadian forces, led by Major General Phineas Riall. This time, the American forces were victorious.

Scott's men were clothed in hastily made gray uniforms, instead of the traditional army blue uniforms. This change in tradition was necessary because of shortages of blue cloth. That first "long gray line" which formed at Chippewa still lives on at the parade ground at West Point. In 1815, in honor of the victory at Chippewa, the United States

War Department ordered that henceforth the dress uniform of the West Point cadets would be made in the style and color of Scott's brigade.

Sixty-Six

On December 19, 1813, British forces crossed the lower Niagara River ("The British Landing," across the road from present-day Stella Niagara Education Park) and proceeded to an easy capture of Fort Niagara.

After that, they soon proceeded to burn every settlement from Lake Ontario to Lake Erie, including Youngstown, Lewiston, Manchester (now a part of the city of Niagara Falls, New York), Black Rock (now a part of the city of Buffalo) and Buffalo. Among the few buildings which were not burnt were a tavern and a number of outhouses.

The reign of terror by the British throughout the American countryside was a direct retaliation for the totally unnecessary burning earlier that December of the village of Newark (now Niagara-on-the-Lake) by American militia led by Brigadier General George McClure.

Spanning the Rapids and the Gorge
Niagara's Bridges

Above Photo: John Penrod

Sixty-Seven

On June 7, 1939, King George VI and Queen Elizabeth, the Queen Mother of Britain, dedicated the site of the Rainbow Bridge, about 500 feet downriver from the location of the Honeymoon Bridge, which was destroyed by ice in 1938. On May 4, 1940, ground was officially broken for the construction of the Rainbow Bridge.

The Rainbow Bridge was built by the Niagara Falls Bridge Commission, an agency formed by the New York State Legislature and the Province of Ontario. Today, the agency also maintains the Lewiston-Queenston and Whirlpool Rapids Bridges.

The cost of the Rainbow Bridge was about $3,760,000. At completion, its 950-foot steel arch was the longest hingeless arch in the world. (Supposedly, the Lewiston-Queenston Bridge, at 1,000 feet, now has that distinction.)

When the two halves of the arch of the Rainbow Bridge were completed, they were off by about one eighth of an inch. The 1,450-foot span of the deck of the bridge is about 202 feet above the lower river. The Rainbow Bridge was formally opened on November 1, 1941, about a month before the United States entered World War II. During the war, the border and bridges between the United States and Canada were carefully guarded.

Sixty-Eight

On Thursday, January 27, 1938, at about 4:15 P.M., a very cold and ominous day, the heavily travelled Honeymoon Bridge, also known as the Upper Steel Arch Bridge or Falls View Bridge, was literally pushed off its abutments by a record 60-foot high ice bridge. Within a mere five seconds, starting at its center, the historic span fell upon the ice, a tangled mass of steel and wood.

Realizing the seriousness of the situation, the bridge was closed the previous day at about 9:15 A.M. Engineers worked frantically in the gorge trying to save it, but the ice was relentless in its accumulating mass and power.

The wreckage lay on the ice until the following April, when most of it sank where it had fallen, while a 250-foot section floated downriver

*The Honeymoon Bridge on the ice bridge after
falling on January 27, 1938.*

and sank below the location of the present-day Schoellkopf Geological Museum, where the river is almost 200 feet deep.

Ice bridges form one or more times just about every winter below the falls. They are made mostly from ice floes which come down from Lake Erie, break up into smaller pieces in the upper rapids, plunge over the falls and then mass together in the lower river from shore to shore.

Sixty-Nine

The first test trip of the Niagara Spanish Aero Car took place on January of 1916. It began carrying as many as 39 passengers on August 8, 1916. The ten minute 1,770-foot trip back and forth 250 feet above the Whirlpool goes from Colt Point to Thomson Point, both in Canada.

It is called the Spanish Aero Car because it was designed by the Spanish engineer, Leonardo Torres Quevedo. The project's cost of about $120,000 was funded by a group of Spanish-capitalists. The original car, built in Balboa, Spain, was replaced in the 1960's.

The setup for the aero car includes seven one-inch stainless steel cables, each attached at the terminals. The ride operates from April to November, averaging about 220,000 passengers each year.

There has never been an accident with the aero car. Even so, there are built-in safeguards, including a rescue car.

Seventy

On June 30, 1898, the Upper Steel Arch Bridge (or Falls View Bridge) was completed. It replaced the Upper Suspension Bridge. It wasn't until its collapse in 1938 that the Upper Steel Arch Bridge became known as the Honeymoon Bridge.

Seventy-One

On the stormy night of January 9-10, 1889, the Upper Suspension Bridge was blown down by a heavy gale. Just before it broke apart, its cables and platforms danced up and down. No one was on the bridge when it fell. It was replaced by a similar but sturdier bridge which opened on May 7 of the same year.

Seventy-Two

On Friday, January 1, 1869, about one-eighth of a mile below the American Falls, the Upper Suspension Bridge was opened. At that time, it was one of the longest suspension bridges in the world, with a span of 1,268 feet. It cost $250,000 to build. It was the first bridge across the gorge and was located fairly close to the falls.

Seventy-Three

Before the first bridge was constructed across the Niagara River gorge, people often crossed from one side to the other by using ferries located in the calmer waters below the falls. In 1847, there was a new way to cross the chasm, for those unafraid of heights. At a cost of $1 each, two people could sit in an iron basket (it looked very much like two rocking chairs joined together) and ride on a secure cable from

Stone Pedestrian Bridge from Green Island to Goat Island.

one country to the other. It must have been quite a thrill to be dangling 190 feet above the wild river.

The cable to which the basket was attached was actually situated where it was because of plans to erect the first suspension bridge across the gorge. How that cable was put in place is quite interesting. A $10 prize was offered to the first person who could fly a kite to the American side of the gorge. The prize was won by 15-year-old Homan Walsh. After his kite string was secured, a rope was pulled across on it, followed by a wire cable. That cable was then followed by heavier and heavier cables.

The bridge erected on the site of the basket ride was designed by Charles Ellet. His Niagara Falls Suspension Bridge opened on August 1, 1848. It was replaced by the Lower Steel Arch Bridge near the turn of the century. The new bridge was actually built around the old one so well that traffic was never impeded. The name of the Lower Steel Arch Bridge was changed to the Whirlpool Rapids Bridge in 1937.

Above Photo: Paul Gromosiak

The American Rapids Bridge as seen from Goat Island.

Seventy-Four

The first bridge to Goat Island was built in 1817. It was made of wood and located where today's American Rapids Bridge spans the rapids. It's builder, Augustus Porter, a local businessman and owner of the island, wanted the bridge there so he could take walks to the island from his house, which was located near the mainland end of the bridge.

In the spring of 1818, ice floes from Lake Erie swept Porter's bridge away. He decided to replace it, but in a better location farther downstream, where the ice floes would be broken up and less hazardous after their trip through the rapids. He built one bridge from the mainland to Green Island and another from Green Island to Goat Island.

In 1856, Porter replaced the wooden bridge to Green Island with one made of iron. In 1858, he placed a similar bridge from Green Island to Goat Island.

In 1900, the State of New York replaced Porter's iron Bridges with the pair of concrete and stone bridges used today by pedestrians and state vehicles.

The American Rapids Bridge was constructed in 1959.

Harnessing the Falls
The Development of Hydroelectric Power

DIVERSION OF WATER FROM LAKE ERIE AND THE NIAGARA RIVER FOR TRANSPORTATION AND PRODUCTION OF HYDROELECTRIC POWER

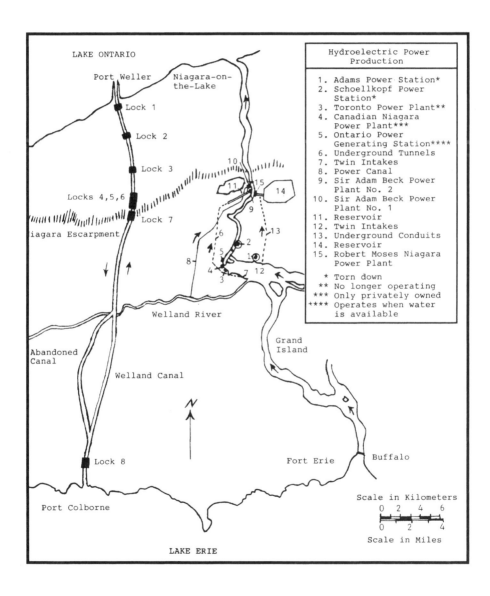

Seventy-Five

Shortly after 5 P.M., on Thursday, June 7, 1956, with a sound like thunder, hundreds of tons of rock, concrete and rubble fell on and destroyed nearly two thirds of the old Schoellkopf Power Station. One worker was killed. The damage was a staggering $100 million. Fortunately, electric power from distant sources soon gave relief to the homes and businesses affected by the disaster.

The Niagara Mohawk Power company, owner of the damaged station, repaired and reopened about one third of the original structure. After the completion of the huge state-owned Robert Moses Power Plant in 1961, the Schoellkopf Power Station was shut down and dismantled.

Today, the Schoellkopf Geological Museum is located above the site of the Schoellkopf Power Station.

Seventy-Six

The International Flow Control Structure was constructed in 1954, about one half of a mile above the Horseshoe Fall. It extended about 1,550 feet from the Canadian shore. To some visitors it looked like an unfinished bridge.

The Control Structure was built for two basic reasons. First, to force water from the upper river into the American Rapids and over the American and Bridal Veil Falls. That was necessary because proposals were made to divert 75% of the upper river to new power plants. Since the bed of the American side of the river is about ten feet higher than the Canadian side, water diversion would naturally drain more water from the American side.

The second reason for building the Control Structure was to divert water from the upper river into the intakes for the American and Canadian power stations.

In 1963, the Control Structure was extended another 650 feet to meet the demands of the new Robert Moses Power Station. Visitors still think the Control Structure looks like an unfinished bridge.

Above Photo From: Schoellkopf Geology Museum

The beginning of the end of most of the Schoellkopf Power Station.

Above Photo From: New York State Parks, Schoellkopf Geology Museum

Schoellkopf Power Generating Station 3 after its collapse due to a rockfall on June 7, 1956 (8 p.m.). Section A (left) was put back into operation. Sections B & C were completely destroyed.

Seventy-Seven

In 1895, the Niagara Falls Power Company began to deliver large amounts of electricity from its Niagara Plant No. 2 (later called the Adams Power Station), located about 7,000 feet above the American Falls. Also that year, the first electrochemical industries began to operate nearby. Niagara Falls, New York, was destined to become known as the Power City of the World.

Seventy-Eight

In 1881, the Niagara Falls Hydraulic Power and Manufacturing Company built its Power Station No. 1 at the top of the gorge, below the American Falls. The station used water sent to it via a canal from the upper river. This was the first time electrical power was produced for commercial use.

Other Footnotes in Falls History

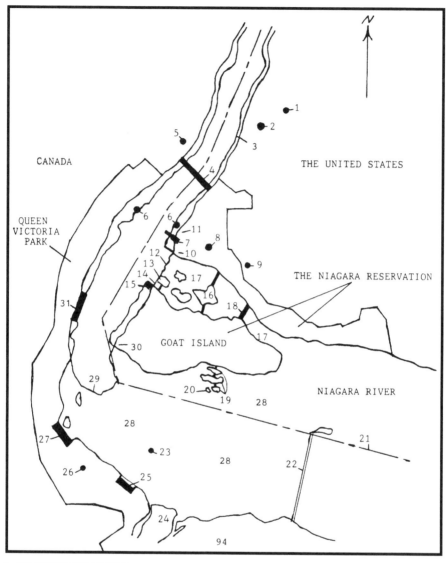

Seventy-Nine

On Friday, March 30, 1990, magician David Copperfield appeared on a CBS television special, "The Niagara Challenge." Copperfield seemed to go over the Horseshoe Falls while chained to a burning raft, and then suddenly emerged from the mist holding on to a rope tied to a helicopter. Of course, the whole act was an illusion.

Eighty

In 1979, scenes from the popular movie, Superman II, featuring Christopher Reeve, as Superman, and Margot Kidder, as Lois Lane, were filmed at Table Rock and by the Whirlpool Rapids, where Superman "rescued" Lois from the violent current.

Eighty-One

In 1981, an efficient system of 18 Xenon lights was installed to light the falls. Each 250,000,000 candlepower light produces the colors white, red, amber, green and blue.

Eighty-Two

In 1956, the first American elm tree afflicted with Dutch Elm disease was found in the Niagara Parks, Canada, Today, the once common tree is quite rare.

Eighty-Three

In 1953, as part of the effort to control erosion and preserve the beauty of the falls, 24,000 cubic yards (18,360 cubic meters) were excavated from the Goat Island flank of the Horseshoe Falls, while 64,000 cubic yards (48,960 cubic meters) were excavated from the Table Rock flank.

Eighty-Four

Around 8:03 P.M., on Sunday, March 22, 1953, a mysterious object exploded over the upper Niagara River. The explosion was preceded by a blinding flash of light. Some people claimed they saw metallic debris floating in the water toward the falls. The authorities never found any physical evidence to explain the incidents, and they surmised that a meteorite had struck the river.

Eighty-Five

The 20th Century-Fox movie, Niagara, starring Marilyn Monroe and Joseph Cotton, was shot entirely on the Canadian side of the Niagara River. Made in 1952, when Marilyn was still dating the famous baseball player, Joe DiMaggio, the movie made Marilyn into a star.

Eighty-Six

In 1936, for the first time ever, the roar of the Horseshoe Falls was heard around the world on a special Christmas radio broadcast.

Eighty-Seven

In June of 1923, a man who purchased a World War I subchaser, the Sunbeam, planned to convert it into a pleasure boat. He and his crew had to get it from New York City to Chicago, via the Erie Canal and Lake Erie. When they reached the lake, they headed north instead of west, going up the Niagara River to Chippewa, Ontario. They were tired, and it was already evening, so they decided to spend the night in the quaint village.

Somehow, during the night, the Sunbeam broke loose from where it had been tied up. It drifted quietly into the Canadian Rapids, where it stopped and turned on its side, close to the scow stranded in 1918.

Above Photo From: Niagara Falls, NY Public Library

Before 1912, people explored the ice bridges below the falls. Note the shantees. They provided refreshments and mementoes.

The owner of the subchaser realized there was nothing he could do to get his boat back. All was not lost, though, when he found a buyer for the craft. William "Red" Hill, Niagara's famous riverman thought he could salvage the Sunbeam. Well, he couldn't.

In a few short years, the mostly wooden boat broke up, leaving behind its motor and a few other metal parts lying on the rocks.

Eighty-Eight

During the Pan-American Exposition at Buffalo in 1901, the American and Horseshoe Falls were illuminated by searchlights. The Whirlpool Rapids and Gorge were also illuminated using a searchlight mounted on one of the electric trolley cars which went up and down the Great Gorge Route. This was the first time all of the falls were illuminated using electric lights.

The illumination at Niagara attracted a lot of the people attending Buffalo's exposition. Among the viewers were their Royal Highnesses the Duke and Duchess of Cornwall and York, Later King George V and Queen Mary.

Eighty-Nine

During the winter of 1888-89, a monstrous ice bridge formed in the gorge. It destroyed the Maid of the Mist docks on both sides of the river, and it nearly pushed the Upper Steel Arch Bridge off its abutments — an omen of things to come?

Ninety

Queen Victoria Park in Ontario officially opened on Victoria Day, May 24, 1888. The park embraces all the land along the river from Clifton Hill to Dufferin Islands. Unlike Niagara Reservation State Park, across the river, the Canadian park has become a series of botanical gardens in a formal park setting.

Ninety-One

On July 15, 1885, with a great deal of fanfare, Niagara Reservation State Park opened, becoming the oldest state park in the United States. Over 750,000 people attended the festivities that day.

The designer of the 300-acre reserve (most of it water) was Frederick Law Olmsted, the landscape architect who designed Central Park in New York City and Delaware Park in Buffalo. He wanted the visitor's experience in the Niagara Reservation to be similar to a walk through the wilderness areas of Yosemite or Yellowstone.

Both Queen Victoria Park and the Niagara Reservation afford fantastic panoramic view of the falls.

Ninety-Two

On September 14, 1860, at about 10 P.M., the Horseshoe Falls was artificially illuminated for the first time. It was done to celebrate the visit of Britain's Prince of Wales.

About 200 Bengal lights (flares with a steady blue light) were placed in three locations on the Canadian side of the river — across from the American Falls, below Table Rock and behind the Horseshoe Fall.

The effect of the flares was quite nice, according to the British press, creating an effect on the falls which was much like light passing through fine crystal.

Ninety-Three

In 1841, the first recorded "photograph" of the falls was taken. It was actually a daguerreotype, a photograph made on a plate of chemically treated metal. The person who made the daguerreotype of the falls was H. L. Patterson, from Newcastle, England.

Ninety-Four

On December 29, 1837, during a period of political turmoil in Canada, known as the Patriot War, a Canadian raiding party crossed the Niagara River at night and took control of the American steamer, Caroline, which the Canadians claimed was being used to take supplies to Navy Island, the headquarters of the rebels.

After everyone was taken off the ship, it was set on fire and released to the currents of the upper river. After passing through the American Rapids, the Caroline became grounded just above the American Falls, where it burnt to the waterline. Some historians argue that one American was killed in the raid.

Above Photo: *Paul Gromosiak*

The elevators to the Cave of the Winds walk.

Ninety-Five

The Cave of the Winds was once a most unique and exciting place. It was a cavern, about 130 feet high, 100 feet wide and 30 feet deep, located behind the Bridal Veil Falls (also known as the Luna Falls). After the piers in the American Rapids were removed in the 1880's, the greater normal flow of water once again went over the Bridal Veil Falls, spreading out about 200 feet at its bottom, making the falls appear like a bride's veil.

The cave was probably first seen by people who rode boats to the foot of Goat Island during the late 1700's and early 1800's. Credit for making the first visit to the cave was given to two local boys, Berry H. White and George W. Sims, who happened upon the cave on July 15, 1834, after they accidentally fell into the dangerous waters below the Bridal Veil Falls. They were able to climb onto the rocks below Luna

Island, from which they noticed that they could walk back to the foot of Goat Island by going behind the Bridal Veil Falls.

The Cave of the Winds was first called Aeolus' Cave, Aeolus being the fabled Greek God of the Winds. It was very windy in the cave, truly "breathtaking." Despite its hazards and discomforts, it became very popular with both tourists and local people.

In the 1860's, to see the cave, each person had to change into special clothing: a skull cap, an oilskin coat, a flannel shirt, flannel drawers, flannel socks and slippers, and cords tied securely around the waist and ankles.

On April 15, 1925, the elevators to the cave were completed. The Biddle Stairs, used to get to the foot of Goat Island and the cave since 1829, were torn down in 1927.

On Labor Day, September 6, 1920, a sudden rockfall of shale crushed three people to death in the cave. Two others were severely injured, and many others had minor injuries. Because of that accident and the possibility of more rockfalls, walks behind the Bridal Veil Falls ended in 1924. From then until 1955, people were allowed to walk up to the cave. That was discontinued in 1956 after the removal of most of the ceiling of the cave. Since that time, people have only been permitted to walk to the base of the Bridal Veil Fall.

From 1970 to 1972, the walk to the base of the Bridal Veil Falls was suspended. The Falls were dried up and work was done to prevent future rockfalls there and at Luna Island.

Every year, the oak walkway of the Cave of the Winds walk has to be dismantled in the fall and reassembled in the spring. That is necessary because of the destructive masses of ice which usually form below the falls in winter.

Ninety-Six

In 1836, the first railroad, with horse-drawn cars, began service between Buffalo and Niagara Falls, New York. This marked the beginning of the end of Niagara Falls as a spa for the wealthier classes. The coming of the railroad made it possible for the lower classes to afford to travel to the falls.

Ninety-Seven

There are a number of towers in the vicinity of the falls today, but there was only one tower that was ever constructed in the rapids at the brink of one of the Niagara Falls. Before the 1950's, the place on Goat Island now called Terrapin Point was known as Terrapin Rocks. Terrapin Rocks was a shallow part of the flank of the Horseshoe Falls, where a large number of rounded boulders looked to some people like the backs of turtles, thus the name.

For a number of years in the early part of the last century, the owner of Goat Island, Augustus Porter, maintained a wooden walkway from the bluff above the Horseshoe Falls out to the end of Terrapin Rocks. The walkway was placed from boulder to boulder, with the rapids flowing between. For awhile, Porter even had a walkway sticking out about ten feet over the misty abyss.

In 1833, Porter erected a 45-foot high stone tower near the end of Terrapin Rocks. It looked a lot like a lighthouse. It became known to many as the Lover's Tower, since so many couples lingered on its parapet. It was actually called Terrapin Tower.

For reasons which are not quite certain, the tower was blasted down with dynamite in 1873. That pleased its critics who thought it looked incongruous by the falls.

Terrapin Rocks became Terrapin Point in the 1950's, when the State of New York placed fill there, creating an artificial viewing area. A couple of the old Terrapin Rocks can still be seen over the railing facing the foot of Goat Island.

Ninety-Eight

On June 18, 1829, Francis Abbott, a tall, thin, intelligent, multitalented and handsome young man, from Plymouth, England, arrived in the village of Niagara Falls, New York. He wore some kind of strange-looking brown cloak. In his left arm, he carried a roll of blankets, a portfolio, a flute, and a large book. With his right hand, he held a cane. He stayed in a few places before settling down in a rude log cabin just north of the American Falls.

While he stayed at Niagara, he acquired a violin, a guitar, a cat and a dog. He often visited the local library and he did a lot of writing and painting, although he always destroyed his creations. Being quite shy, he only became the acquaintance of one person, Judge Samuel DeVeaux, a prominent local businessman.

Abbott roamed around mostly at night, often playing one of his instruments. His favorite haunt was Goat Island. He had two favorite places for bathing. One was a small cascade by the first of the Three Sisters Islands. Today that place is called the Hermit's Cascade, in memory of Abbott.

Francis' other bathing spot was below the American Falls, near the shore. That was not a wise place to bathe. On June 10, 1831, around 2 P.M., he was seen there by a few people. He was never seen alive again. His body was found near Fort Niagara ten days later. He was buried in an unmarked grave. Francis, the Hermit of Niagara, will forever remain one of Niagara's most popular mysteries.

Ninety-Nine

On November 27, 1829, the first Welland Canal opened, taking vessels from the upper Niagara River, at Chippewa, to Lake Ontario, at Port Dalhousie. Through the years, the canal route has been changed; each time the depth and width were increased. Today's canal crosses the Niagara Peninsula from Port Colborne to Port Dalhousie and it is a vital link of the St. Lawrence Seaway System, which allows ships from all over the world to travel through all the Great Lakes, avoiding the Niagara River's rapids and falls.

One Hundred

In 1827, Thomas Barnett built a stone house near Table Rock and later converted it into the first museum by the falls. His extensive collection and more recent additions were housed in the Niagara Falls Museum, located just north of the Rainbow Bridge in Niagara Falls, Ontario, before it was closed.

One Hundred-One

In 1818, the same man who named the Three sisters Islands, Parkhurst Whitney, constructed the first real stairway down to the river's edge, below Prospect Point. That same year, he and William Forsythe began a rowboat ferry service across the river below the falls.

Bibliography

Aug, Lisa, *Beyond the Falls, a Modern History of the Lower Niagara River.* Niagara Falls, New York: Niagara Books, 1992

Bannon, Anthony, et al. *Arcadia Revisted, Niagara River and Falis from Lake Erie to Lake Ontario.* Albuquerque: University of New Mexico Press, 1988

Benson, Adolph B., Ed. *Peter Kalm's Travels in North America.* New York: Dover Publications, Inc. 1937

Berton, Pierre. *Niagara, a History of the Falls.* Toronto: McClelland & Stewart, Inc., 1992

Bingham, Robert W. *Niagara, Highway of Heroes.* Buffalo: Foster and Stewart Publishing Corporation, 1943

Bowler, R. Arthur, Ed. *War along the Niagara, Essays on the War of 1812 and Its Legacy.* Youngstown, New York: Old Fort Niagara Association, Inc., 1991

Braider, Donald. *The Niagara.* New York: Holt, Rinehart and Winston, 1972

Broughton, J. G., et al. *Geology of New York; a Short Account.* Albany: The University of the State of New York, 1966

Campbell, Jane Cannon. *Frontier Aflame.* Interlaken, New York: Heart of the Lakes Publishing, 1987

Colden, Cadwallader. *The History of the Five Indian Nations Depending on the Province of New-York in America, 1727, 1747.* Ithaca: Cornell University Press, 1964

DeVeaux, Samuel. *The Falls of Niagara or Tourists' Guide to This Wonder of Nature.* Buffalo: Press of Thomas and Company, 1839

Donaldson, Gordon. *Niagara! The Eternal Circus.* New York: Doubleday & Company, Inc., 1926

Douglass, Harry S., et al. *History of Northwestern New York; Erie, Niagara, Wyoming, Genesee and Orleans Counties.* New York: Lewis Historical Publishing Company, Inc., 1947, Volume 2

Dow, Charles Mason. *Anthology and Bibliography of Niagara Falls.* Albany: The State of New York, 1921, 2 volumes

Dow, Charles Mason. *The State Reservation at Niagara, a History.* Albany: J. B. Lyon Company, 1914

Drescher, Nuala McGann. *Engineers for the Public Good: a History of the Buffalo District U.S. Army Corps of Engineers.*

Dunnigan, Brian Leigh. *Glorious Relic, the French Castle and Old Fort Niagara.* Youngstown, New York: Old Fort Niagara Association, Inc., 1987

Dunnigan, Brian Leigh. *Old Fort Niagara in Four Centuries, a History of Its Development.* Youngstown, New York: Old Fort Niagara Association, Inc., 1991

Dunnigan, Brian Leigh. *Siege — 1759, the Campaign Against Niagara.* Youngstown, New York: Old Fort Niagara Association, Inc., 1986 Edwards, C. R. A Story of Niagara. Buffalo: Breed, Lent & Company, 1870

Fairchild, Herman L. *Geology of Western New York.* Rochester: Fairchild, Herman L., 1925

Forrester, Glenn C. *Niagara Falls and the Glacier.* Hicksville: Exposition Press, 1976

Fryer, Mary Beacock. *Battlefields of Canada. Toronto:* Dundurn Press, 1986

Gardner, James T., Director. *Special Report of New York State Survey on the Preservation of the Scenery of Niagara Falls.* Albany: Charles Van Benthuysen L Sons, 1880

Gayler, Hugh J., Ed. *Niagara's Changing Landscapes.* Ottawa: Carleton University Press, 1994

Graham, Lloyd. *Niagara Country.* New York: Duell, Sloan & Pearce, 1949

Greenhill, Ralph, and Mahoney, Thomas D. *Niagara.* Toronto: University of Toronto Press, 1969

Gromosiak, Paul. *Niagara Falls Q/A, Answers to the 100 Most Common Questions About Niagara Falls.* Buffalo: Western New York Wares Inc., 1989

Gromosiak, Paul. *Soaring Gulls and Bowing Trees, the History of the Islands Above Niagara Falls.* Buffalo: Western New York Wares Inc., 1989

Gromosiak, Paul. *Zany Niagara, the Funny Things People Say About Niagara Falls.* Buffalo: Western New York Wares Inc., 1992

Hamilton, Edward P., Ed. *Adventure in the Wilderness, the American Journals of Louis Antoine De Bougainville, 1756-1760.* University of Oklahoma Press, 1964

Holley, George W. *Niagara: Its History and Geology, Incidents and Poetry.* New York: Sheldon and Company, 1872

Howard, Robert West. *Thundergate: the Forts of Niagara.* Englewood Cliffs, New Jersey: Prentice-Hall, 1968

Howells, W. D., Twain, Mark, et al. *The Niagara Book.* New York: Doubleday, Page & Company, 1901

Hulbert, Archer Butler. *The Niagara River.* New York: G. P. Putnam's Sons, 1908

Lane, Christopher W. *Impressions of Niagara, the Charles Rand Penney Collection of Prints of Niagara Falls and the Niagara River from the Sixteenth to the Early Twentieth Centuries.* Philadelphia: The Philadelphia Print Shop, Ltd., 1993

Lewis, J. C., Ed. *Guide to the Natural History of the Niagara Region.* St. Catherines: J. C. Lewis, 1991

MacLean, Harrison John. *The Fate of the Griffon.* Chicago: The Swallow Press Inc., 1974

McGreevy, Patrick V. *Imagining Niagara, the Meaning and Making of Niagara Falls.* Amherst: University of Massachusetts Press, 1994

McKinsey, Elizabeth. *Niagara Falls, Icon of the American Sublime.* Cambridge: Cambridge University Press, 1985

Morgan, Lewis Henry. *League of the Hodenosaunee, Iroquois.* New York: Sage & Brother, Publishers, 1851

Oppel, Frank, Ed. New York, *Tales of the Empire State.* Secaucus: Castle, 1988

Peckham, Howard H. *The Colonial Wars: 1689-1762.* Chicago: The University of Chicago Press, 1964

Pool, William. *Landmarks of Niagara County.* D. Mason & Company, 1897

Porter, Peter A. *Official Guide, Niagara Falls, River, Frontier.* Buffalo: The Matthews Northrup Works, 1901

Pouchot, Pierre. *Memoirs on the Late War in North America Between France and England.* Youngstown, New York: Old Fort Niagara Association, Inc., 1994

Richter, Daniel K. *The Ordeal of the Longhouse, the Peoples of the Iroquois League in the Era of European Colonization.* Chapel Hill:

University of North Carolina Press, 1992 Robson, Margaret D. *Under the Mountain.* Buffalo: Henry Stewart, Inc., 1958

Seibel, George A. *Bridges over the Niagara Gorge, Rainbow Bridges — 50 Years: 1941-1991.* Niagara Falls, ontario: Niagara Falls Bridge Commission, 1991

Seibel, George A. *The Niagara Portage Road, a History of the Portage on the West Bank of the Niagara River.* Niagara falls, Ontario: The City of Niagara Falls, Ontario, 1990

Seibel, George A. *Ontario's Niagara Parks, 100 Years.* Niagara Falls, Ontario: The Niagara Parks Commission, 1985

Severance, Frank H. *An Old Frontier of France.* New York: Dodd, Mead and company, 1917

Swiggett, Howard. *War Out of Niagara.* New York: Columbia University Press, 1933

Tesmer, Irving H., Ed. *Colossal Cataract, the Geologic History of Niagara Falls.* Albany: State of New York Press, 1981

Tiplin, Albert H. *Our Romantic Niagara, a Geological History of the River and the Falls.* Niagara Falls, Ontario: The Niagara Falls Heritage Foundation, 1988

Todish, Timothy J. *America's First First World War.* Grand Rapids: Suagothel Productions Ltd., 1982

Turner, O. *Pioneer History of the Holland Purchase of Western New York.* Buffalo: George H. Derby & Company, 1850

Van Diver, Bradford B. *Upstate New York.* Dubuque: Kendall/Hunt Publishing Company, 1980

Vinal, Theodora, *Niagara Portage, from Past to Present.* Buffalo: Henry Stewart, Inc., 1955

Vogel, Michael N. *Echoes in the Mist, an Illustrated History of the Niagara Falls Area.* Chatsworth: Windsor Publications, Inc., 1991

Williams, Edward Theodore. *Niagara, Queen of Wonders.* Boston: Chapple Publishing Company, Ltd., 1916